Rev. Donald C. Swope Ⓕ

T 25

D1370655

bible studies
on marriage and the family
for couples and groups

two
become
one

j. allan petersen

with

elven and joyce smith

TYNDALE HOUSE PUBLISHERS   wheaton, illinois

COVERDALE HOUSE PUBLISHERS LTD.   london, england

Library of Congress Catalog Card Number 72-97660
ISBN 8423-7620-8

Copyright © 1973 by Family Concern, Inc. of United
States of America. All rights reserved. No part
of this book may be reproduced in any form without
written permission of Family Concern, Inc.

Seventh printing, December 1976

Printed in the United States of America

contents

preface

There are few couples, with an already overloaded schedule, who could work together with me on a penetrating study on marriage and still come up more happily married than ever.

Elven and Joyce Smith have done it. They are key representatives of the Navigators in California, and this alone is a big enough challenge for any man and wife. But they spent dozens of hours on this project at home, during vacation, in motel rooms, and wherever precious minutes could be stolen from something else. They were equal to the opportunity and were stretched bigger in the process. They are an uncommon pair, with an uncommon concern for other couples.

In a day when there is more education against marriage and family life than for it, this study serves a significant purpose. It brings into clear focus the biblical teaching on these important subjects and in a form where they can be easily grasped and retained.

Any study exclusively for husbands or wives regarding their peculiar roles is good. One for both partners is better. It enables a couple to learn together, and this in itself encourages understanding and communication. It also provides a warm atmosphere for healthy self-discovery and improvement. The two who are already one will learn how to make this oneness a reality in practice.

J. Allan Petersen
Omaha, Nebraska

how to get the most from this study

"For the Lord gives wisdom; from his mouth come knowledge and understanding" Proverbs 2:6, RSV.

This series of studies has been designed to help you search the Scriptures for answers to questions about marriage and the family.

It is intended for use by the following:

1. *An individual,* who will find it helpful in strengthening the marriage from one partner's side.

2. *A couple,* who can share their findings as they work through a lesson together. It may be preferable, however, because of time pressures, for partners to do a lesson individually, then set aside a time to share their answers, reactions, and applications gained from that particular lesson.

3. *A small group,* composed of several couples, who prepare a lesson beforehand, and then come together to discuss it. Maximum benefit from *Two Become One* is derived from the interaction that occurs in these small groups where couples can learn from one another as they seek to deepen their marriage relationships.

4. *A Sunday school class,* who can complete the lessons in one 13-week Sunday school quarter, by assigning the material weekly to be done as homework. The Sunday school class could be led by the regular teacher, or divided into smaller interaction groups with a leader assigned to guide each one.

Each partner should have his own copy of *Two Become One.* You need only a Bible and a pen to begin! Occasionally a dictionary will be needed. Each question will direct you to a passage of Scripture. After reading the passage, write the answer in your own words. References are given in this way: Ephesians 5:21. This means the book of Ephesians, chapter 5, verse 21.

Be sure to pray and ask the Lord for understanding as you do each lesson. Set aside a regular time to work on your study, allowing an hour or so to complete the lesson. Some lessons are longer than others. It may be best for you to take a few questions each day instead of trying to finish the lesson all at one time.

There are three questions to keep in mind as you do each study:

What does it *say?*
What does it *mean?*
What am I to *do* about it?

Unless you *apply* the Scriptures to your life, there is little value in knowing what it says—but when you obey God's Word you will see growth in your life and your marriage. Questions have been placed in each lesson to help you make an application of that study to your life. It is important to do these and occasionally to check previous applications to see how you are progressing in making needed changes.

a word to leaders

Each lesson is carefully worked out so that a leader can easily guide a group discussion. The leader should have those in his group discuss the facts learned in each section of the lesson, share what they understand it to mean, and relate what personal application can then be drawn.

He should encourage interaction by making sure that everyone has an opportunity to share, rather than allowing one person or couple to monopolize the conversation. Require and expect that each person complete the lesson before the discussion time. Remember that the Bible is the source book for this study and unless an opinion question is asked, the answer the Bible gives is the one expected.

Insight may be gained from reading other books (recommended reading is *The Marriage Affair* by J. Allan Petersen, since it covers each of the topics in the lessons) but keep the teachings of God's Word as the basis for expecting God to help "Two Become One."

beginnings for marriage

"I now declare you to be man and wife!"

When this pronouncement is made, the marriage *ceremony* ends and the marriage *life* begins!

In their wedding vows, a man and a woman commit themselves to the mutual responsibility and challenge of sharing life together, "no longer two but one."

Each partner desires to have a happy and satisfying marriage—a worthy goal shared by most couples of any age or at any stage of married life.

The fulfillment a husband or wife expects to receive from this intimate relationship may be greatly influenced by the *reasons* they had for wanting to be married.

motivation

Both sexes share common reasons but their order of importance may vary.

1. List below what you think some of these reasons are for men and women.

Why women marry   Why men marry

_____   _____   _____   _____

_____   _____   _____   _____

_____   _____   _____   _____

_____   _____   _____   _____

_____ _____   _____ _____

_____ _____   _____   _____

2. As you anticipated marriage, which of the reasons above were especially important to you?

_____

_____

_____

3. Which reasons do you feel were of prime importance to your mate?

_____

_____

_____

the scriptures

The Scriptures contain clear teaching about marriage and family life. When you follow these instructions and principles given by God (who ordained marriage in the first place), then you can build the kind of relationships which give personal fulfillment and provide a solid, happy, and well-functioning family unit.

See what insight you can gain from the following passages. There will be further study on some of these in later lessons.

1. Read Genesis 2:18-25. Give particular thought to verses 18, 23, and 24 and then answer the following:

A. Who said it was not good that man should be alone?

_____

B. Loneliness is the first thing which God named "not good." What did he do about it?

_____

_____

C. What do you understand the word "helper" or "help meet" to mean?

_____

_____

_____

D. The Revised Standard Version of the Bible translates verse 23: "This *at last* is bone of my bones and flesh of my flesh; she shall be called Woman, because she was taken out of Man."

How would you describe Adam's response to the Lord God bringing Eve to him?

_____

_____

_____

E. The following statements relate to verse 24. Mark these true or false.

a. _____ A man is to assume independent responsibility for his wife.

b. _____ God designed marriage to be a permanent union.

c. _____ Each partner in the marriage is complete in herself/himself.

2. The book of Proverbs contains a collection of wise sayings about the whole of life.

A. What does Proverbs 18:22 say about the choice of a wife?

_____

_____

_____

B. What further insight can be gained from Proverbs 19:14?

_____

_____

_____

_____

_____

3. What instruction was given to man at the beginning of history regarding procreation? Genesis 1:27, 28.

_____

_____

_____

4. God, speaking through Paul in Ephesians 5:21-33 indicates how the marriage relationship is to reflect the relationship which exists between Christ and the Church, his redeemed bride.

A. What does verse 21 say to you?

_____

_____

_____

B. How can the wife help her husband assume his position of leadership? Verses 22, 24.

_____

_____

C. How are husbands admonished to love their wives? Verses 25-28.

_____

_____

D. In what ways can a husband abuse his position as head of the wife?

_____

_____

_____

foundations

The existence of the family rests on many foundations and the responsible couple will give careful attention to establishing right ones. Building a Christian home is an art.

The experiences each one has within the family prepare him for the encounters he will have in the wider circles of life, thus the importance of laying sound foundations becomes even greater.

The following statements in quotes are comments (paraphrased) that the Bible makes about the importance of right foundations:

1. Matthew 7:24-27—"If a house (home-marriage) is to endure the storms of life it must be built on a solid foundation."

In your opinion, what essentials go into a solid foundation for marriage?

_____

_____

_____

_____

_____

_____

2. Psalm 11:3—"A good life has to be established on good foundations and if these are destroyed what can develop?"

What are things that erode the foundation of marriage?

_____

_____

_____

_____

1 Corinthians 3:10-15 says, "If we expect to have a good building, we not only have to have the right foundation but must also use the right materials in building on it."

14

In succeeding lessons we will be digging into and discussing what the foundation and building materials are and how these are utilized.

application

The marriage cannot be changed without changing the people in it. Marriage is not primarily an institution but two people who are sharing a *life*. Happiness in this life is not so much finding the right person, as *being* the right person!

1. As you evaluate your own marriage, discuss the things each of you likes about your marriage as it is now. Jot them down.

_____

_____

_____

_____

_____

2. Talk about and then write down one thing you are going to work on now to help strengthen your marriage.

_____

_____

_____

3. How do you plan to put this into practice?

_____

_____

summary

People marry for a variety of reasons. It is important to know, understand, and try to meet the needs of your mate. You need to talk together about these things—where they fit with you and what the Bible has to say about them. Then you need to realize that you can grow and build together, with the right materials, toward a successful marriage.

lesson 2

what is this thing called love?

What is the mystique called "love"? That thing "the world needs now"? What has caused men to fight duels, abdicate thrones, conquer worlds, and do a thousand other things?

Many people do not have an adequate understanding of the meaning of the word "love." Another problem is knowing how to demonstrate love in everyday relationships.

love defined

Someone has said that love is not definable, just livable—but try:

1. What do you think? Write your own definition of "love."

_____

_____

_____

_____

_____

2. What does your dictionary say? (If possible, get a contrast between old and new dictionaries.)

_____

_____

_____

_____

_____

3. Our English word "love" is used to convey many different ideas. We speak of "loving" ice cream, dogs, God, and people. As we hear the word in context, we ascribe proper meaning to it. The Greek language, with its four words for love, opens the possibility of a finer categorization.

These words and their definitions are listed below:

A. *Stergo*: A love that is inherent in one's own nature. It is an instinctive, natural affection or protectiveness, such as animal protectiveness for its offspring. It is the love of parents for children and children for parents, of husband for wife and wife for husband, of close relations one for another—just because of the relationship. There is a sense of responsibility for the welfare and well-being of another because of obligation in the natural, not moral, sense. This kind of love is the binding factor by which any natural or social unit is held together.

Examples of *stergo* love would be seen in a father providing for the family and a mother caring for sick members. It is evidenced in the protectiveness of a father toward any threat to his family and in the reluctance of a mother to let her children grow up and become independent of her.

What are some other examples of *stergo* love?

_____

_____

_____

_____

B. *Eros*: A desire for someone for what fulfills one's own selfish desires with little or no regard for the other; it can be passion seeking satisfaction. *Eros'* basis is primarily in the physical, triggered by emotion, and can be good or bad. This is the very heart of sexual desire and romantic infatuation. *Eros* is a selfish love, love turned inward, and always wants something in return for its self-giving.

There is a proper physical, sexual basis to human love which can act as reinforcing steel does to concrete to help build a strong, solid marriage relationship. Physical desire and fulfillment have a true and meaningful place when tempered and balanced by the elements found in the types of love described in 3 and 4, below.

What place does "romantic" love have in the development of your marriage?

_____

_____

_____

_____

_____

_____

C. *Phileo*: A love which is the response of the human spirit to what appeals to it as pleasurable. It is based upon an inner communion and a mutual attraction between the person loving and the person loved. Both have things in common with each other—a similarity of outlook on life. The one loving finds a reflection of his own nature in the person loved. *Phileo* is a love of "liking" and "fondness"—a going out of the heart in delight to that which affords pleasure. The Greeks made much of friendship and this word was used by them to designate mutual affection, as we feel toward a person who is "fun to be with." *Phileo* quality of love is important in marriage simply because we need to like someone and what he is and does. Without it, living with him in an enduring relationship would be untenable.

Give a few examples of how *phileo* fits in your home and marriage.

_____

_____

_____

_____

_____

_____

_____

D. *Agape*: A love called out of one's heart by an awakened sense of value in the object loved that causes one to prize it. This love does not seek anything in return, not even acceptance of itself, but rather is first concerned for the other. It is a self-sacrificing love and in its absolute form denotes God's love —not human love. *Agape* is the rich word used predominately in the New Testament to describe the love of God toward men (John 3:16), and that love which Christians are to have for each other, as illustrated by the love a man has for his wife (Ephesians 5:25). In the Christian sense, it is a spontaneous, uncaused, self-giving love. The crucifixion of Christ is regarded as the supreme manifestation of God's love in that Christ died for helpless, sinful, unworthy man (Romans 5:5-8).

While *eros* love is often motivated by "What can I get?" *agape* love is motivated by "What can I give?" and finds "it is more blessed to give than to receive."

Do you see evidences of *agape* love in your marriage? Explain.

_____

_____

_____

_____

_____

_____

_____

Obviously we cannot split love into four independent segments for these are not necessarily exclusive of each other, but there is an interplay of all in most experiences of love.

love illustrated

Having faced the difficulties of defining what love is, we recognize that love is more than a thing or an emotion. Love is a creative force which is revealed in action.

This lesson should challenge your thinking as to how you can better express your love and fulfill your responsibilities as one who loves.

The Bible defines love by an action.

1. What did God's love prompt him to do as recorded in John 3:16?

_____

_____

2. How was God's love shown to us according to Romans 5:8?

_____

_____

_____

3. 1 Corinthians 13 has been called the love (*agape*) chapter of the New Testament. Verses 4-7 list nine ingredients of what someone has called the "spectrum of love." Consider each one and then give an illustration of how you feel these apply in your marriage and/or family.

A. Love suffers long—patience.

_____

_____

_____

_____

B. Is kind—kindness.

_____

_____

_____

_____

C. Envies not—generosity.

_____

_____

_____

_____

D. Does not vaunt itself, is not puffed up—humility.

_____

_____

_____

_____

E. Does not behave itself unseemly—courtesy.

_____

_____

_____

_____

F. Seeks not her own—unselfishness.

_____

_____

_____   _____

_____

G. Is not easily provoked—good tempered.

_____

_____

_____

_____

H. Thinks no evil—guilelessness.

_____

_____

_____

I. Rejoices not in iniquity but in truth—sincerity.

_____

_____

_____

application

It's easy to agree with all the platitudes and think to yourself, "Yes, that's a good deal, all right!" But how about you? Think back through the things in this section. Which one do you need to work on most?

What is one practical day-by-day way you can do this?

What form of check-up are you planning to insure you do it?

summary

There are eternal lessons for everyone in how to be a more loving person.

Love is more than the sum of its components. It is not static but dynamic and as such must grow and mature or it will diminish through neglect. Generally speaking, people do not "fall in love" but grow into love! "In a word, as God's dear children, try to be like him, and live in love as Christ loved you, *and gave himself up on your behalf* as an offering and sacrifice whose fragrance is pleasing to God" (Ephesians 5:1, 2 New English Bible).

Perhaps the opposite of love is not hate, but self!

lesson 3

accepting yourself
and your partner

Marriage offers a wonderful opportunity for
two people to give love, approval, and understanding to one another.

No other personal relationship calls for the
depth of intimacy and commitment that marriage
does. A husband and wife can encourage each
other's sense of worth, uniqueness, and strength.
How sad, then, that many couples live together for
years without true understanding and so fail in
the basic oneness intended by God for the marital
life.

self-acceptance

A person with any degree of honesty knows he
has done wrong things, needs forgiveness, and has
much room for improvement in his life. However,
it is also true that unless you have a healthy
self-love you cannot adequately love others!

1. The Bible clearly states that a man has a relationship to himself
as well as to God and others.
Read how Jesus expressed this in Matthew 22:35-40, then answer
the following.

A. What should one's attitude be towards himself? Verse 39

_____

B. The normal human tendency seems to be to put self first
and let God and "others" fit into life as it is convenient. Another popular view is that one should love God first, others

next, and self last. But Jesus gives the proper sequence in verses 37-39. What is it?

First _____

Second _____

Third _____

C. Why do you think this is a necessary order?

_____

_____

_____

_____

The mental picture you carry of yourself greatly affects your attitudes, emotions, and responses towards God, family, friends, job, and many other significant areas of your life.

2. What does 2 Corinthians 10:12 indicate is an unwise standard for measuring your self-worth?

_____

_____

3. 1 Samuel 16:7 reveals why the knowledge other people have of you is often based on incomplete information.

A. What is the reason given?

_____

_____

_____

B. In contrast, what further insight does God have about you?

_____

_____

_____

4. There are other factors besides one's appearance that might be used to incorrectly place value upon someone's worth. Identify them as you look up these Scriptures.

A. Matthew 13:55, 56 _____

B. John 1:45, 46 _____

_____

C. Jeremiah 9:23, 24 _____

_____

5. Another reason for a feeling of unworthiness can be found in Luke 15:21. What attitude is expressed in this verse and why?

_____

_____

_____

_____

6. What kind of self-image did you have as a teen-ager? Using the scale 1 as good, 2 as fair, and 3 as poor, how would you have rated yourself in each area?

A. I felt _____ about my parentage.

B. I felt _____ about my appearance.

C. I felt _____ about my abilities.

D. I felt _____ about my environment.

E. I felt _____ about my relationship to God.

Self-esteem is not based on the great things you've accomplished, the mark you've made, the things you own. Nor is it cancelled by your faults, failures, and sins. These acts reveal *what* you are but do not indicate *who* you are and your Divine origin. Self-love and self-approval are not the same.

The true basis for a healthy self-love is to understand and accept the value God places on you!

7. What do the Scriptures say about your worth before God?

A. John 3:16 _____

_____

_____

B. 1 Peter 5:7 _____

_____

_____

C. Jeremiah 31:3 _____

_____

_____

D. John 15:9 _____

_____

_____

Man is unique! God simply spoke and the whole universe came into being through his creative word. He did not speak man into existence, but with special care he personally formed him and endowed him with many of his own divine characteristics.

God did not create any superior or inferior people. There are only different people. Abilities and capacities differ; each person has unique strengths which enable him to make his special contribution to God's plan.

To refuse to accept yourself as God made you is unconscious rebellion and is accusing him of making a mistake. Any kind of rebellion must be honestly faced and confessed.

8. Genesis 1:27 states that God created man in his

_____

9. What marred this image? See Romans 5:12 for your answer.

_____

_____

10. Read Colossians 1:15-22. From verses 20-22 tell in a few words how God restored man to fellowship with himself.

_____

_____

_____

_____

_____

11. God desires that those who come to him should be conformed to the image of (be like) his Son. You can accept a self that is in the process of being made like Jesus! What does each of the references below say about this?

A. 2 Corinthians 3:18 _____

_____

_____

B. Colossians 3:10 _____

_____

_____

C. 2 Peter 1:4 _____

_____

_____

D. 1 John 3:2, 3 _____

_____

_____

The very fact that God, knowing *what* you are, provided Christ for your forgiveness, proves that you are not worthless! Unworthy, yes—but never worthless. His love indicates *who* you are—one of God's important creatures in whom he has a great investment. If God so loved you, you must be a very important person!

12. Being created in God's image you have intellect, emotion, and

a will, which God housed in the body which would best achieve the purpose he has for you.

The Psalmist recognized that every man is a unique creation of God. Using Psalm 139:13-16 list how God specifically designed you.

_____

_____

_____

_____

_____

_____

Thank God you are you!

Commit yourself to God. When you voluntarily give yourself to God for his control and use, you are recognizing your tremendous worth. You are loving yourself in the highest sense of the word.

It is not only safe, but necessary, to love whom God loves—yourself!

understanding your partner

When you are able to accept yourself you will find you are better able to understand and be sensitive to the needs of your mate (Ephesians 5:28).

1. What commandment did Jesus give about loving others? John 13:34, 35.

_____

_____

2. If you focus on the negatives in your partner's life, your love will be weakened. It is God's will that partners love one another. He

will even restore lost love if you follow the remedy given in Philippians 4:8. What does this verse say your thoughts should dwell on?

_____

_____

_____

_____

_____

3. According to Romans 14:10-13 if your partner is a Christian, he is responsible to God. What does this verse caution you against doing?

_____

_____

_____

_____

4. How can you best help your partner as seen in the following verses?

A. 1 Peter 4:8 _____

_____

_____

B. James 5:16 _____

(1) _____

_____

You have been thinking through much Scripture in this lesson. All these verses are important and can make a significant difference in your marriage.

Which one (ones) impressed you most?

_____

How can you begin to apply this to your life?

_____

_____

_____

As you contemplate studying the subject of Christian marriage for several weeks, you may be asking, "How does one become a Christian?" or "How can I know for sure that I am a Christian?" Good questions!

Here is a brief explanation and illustration to help answer these questions.

God made us with both a God-consciousness and the capability to live in a right relationship with God. Although there are a lot of good people, no one is perfect. The Bible describes this simply in Romans 3:23: "All have sinned, and come short of the glory of God." Since sin separates (whether it be in relationship to God or to people) we live in a state of spiritual death. Romans 6:23: "For the wages of sin is death." Because God loves us and desires us to live in right relationship and fellowship with himself, he made a provision for that sin. 1 Peter 3:18: "Christ also hath once suffered for sins, the just for the unjust, that he might bring us to God." Romans 5:8 puts it this way, "God shows his love for us in that while we were yet sinners Christ died for us" (RSV).

The following illustration shows this clearly and depicts 1 Timothy 2:5 as stated in *The Living Bible*: "God is on one side and all the people on the other side; Jesus Christ is between to bring them together."

| MAN — imperfect, sinful, destined for spiritual death (eternal separation from God)

Man's efforts fall short
Ephesians 2:8, 9—"For by grace are ye saved through faith; and that not of yourselves: it is the gift of God: not of works, lest any man should boast." | JESUS — the way across
John 3:16 — "For God so loved the world, that he gave his only begotten Son, that whosoever believeth in him should not perish, but have everlasting life." | GOD — holy, pure, perfect, with a perfect place prepared for us—along with an abundant life while we are here on earth.
John 10:10b — "I am come that they might have life, and that they might have it more abundantly." |

1 ————————➤ 2 ————————➤ 3 ————————➤ 4

The numbers above depict groups of people.

Group one includes everyone; "*All* have sinned."

Group two indicates a progression, the recognition that there probably is a God, but not doing anything about it.

Groups three and *four* are described by one verse, John 1:12: "But as many as received him, to them God gives the right to become his children, even to those who believe on his name."

Group three is made up of those who *believe*. That is, they acknowledge their sin, their need of a Savior, and the fact that Jesus is God in the flesh, who died for them. Many people are in this group but they have never taken the step into *group four*— those who *believe and receive* Christ as Savior. Receiving is an act of the will whereby one invites Jesus Christ into his life as Savior and Lord. How is this done? Revelation 3:20 states, "Behold, I stand at the door and knock, if any man hear my voice and open the door, I will come in to him and will fellowship with him and he with me." It's by personal choice and invitation.

Where do you place yourself in this progression?

If you've never invited Christ into your life or are not sure that you are a Christian, just pray this prayer:

Lord Jesus, I'm a sinner. I know you died for my sins, and I now ask that you come into my life as my Savior and Lord. I know that when you do this, you give me your life. Thank you.

If you did this, sign your name and date it so you can look back on the exact time you became a Christian. Now, on the basis of God's Word you can *know* that you have eternal life! "And what is it that God has said? That he has given us eternal life, and that this life is in his Son. So whoever has God's Son has life; whoever does not have his Son, does not have life. I have written this to you who believe in the Son of God so that you may know you have eternal life" 1 John 5:11-13 *The Living Bible.*

Your Name _____

Date _____

lesson 4

communications

Happily married people communicate well!

The heart of marital "oneness" is the communication system: thus the ability to communicate well is a fundamental skill essential to the growth of the marriage relationship.

Although strong marriages tend to have the same problem areas as weak ones, those marriages which succeed apparently do so because the mates are communicating clearly.

ways to communicate

People communicate in a variety of ways. *Words* are one means by which a person can express himself. *Action* language is another. *Silence* can convey a wealth of information! *Listening* is an indispensable condition for meaningful communication.

1. Following the examples given, list other ways you communicate verbally and non-verbally with your mate.

Verbally	Non-Verbally
Example A. Soft Voice	Example A. With Eyes
B. _____	B. _____
C. _____	C. _____
D. _____	D. _____
E. _____	E. _____

2. How do you think the five senses are involved in what is communicated between marriage partners?

A. Sight _____

_____

_____

_____

B. Hearing _____

_____

_____

_____

C. Touch _____

_____

_____

_____

D. Smell _____

_____

_____

_____

E. Taste _____

_____

why communicate?

Communicate: "To give or interchange thoughts, feelings, information, or the like, by writing, speaking, etc." *Random House Dictionary of the English Language.*

You cannot *not* communicate! Relating to your mate takes place by communication.

1. There are a number of levels of communication. Some of these are listed below. After each one, describe a specific instance which occurred in your home last week.

A. Casual conversation as friends.

B. Sharing of information.

C. Self-disclosure—sharing of feelings, attitudes, emotions with partner.

_____

_____

_____

D. Goal planning (short or long term).

_____

_____

_____

E. Expressions of disagreement, argument.

_____

_____

_____

F. Giving support and encouragement to the other.

_____

_____

_____

G. Listening to partner.

_____

Marriage is intended to be an intimate relationship built upon mutual understanding between husband and wife. For this communion of heart to occur, conversation must go beyond the level of "home and children" to include a sharing of thought and feelings in the experiences of daily living. Do you communicate on all of these levels?

Yes _____ No _____

the art of verbal communication

Consider the immense power of the spoken word for good or bad! It is easy to see why the Bible speaks so often concerning the importance of proper use of the tongue.

Understanding and applying these passages can improve your ability to communicate verbally with your spouse.

1. Examine Ephesians 4:15. From the listing below check the answers you feel are correct.

A. ( ) It doesn't make much difference what you say as long as it is said lovingly.
B. ( ) *How* you say something is important.
C. ( ) "White lies" have a place in communication in marriage.
D. ( ) What and how you speak has a direct effect on maturing in Christ.

2. Ephesians 4:29 gives four principles concerning communication. Can you agree with the two given and list the other two?

A. Don't speak wrongly to or of the other partner.

Yes _____ No _____

B. What you say should help, not hinder, your mate.

Yes _____ No _____

C. _____

_____

D. _____

_____

3. What do the following passages say about *constructive* communication?

Example:
A. Isaiah 50:4 Be an encourager _____

B. Ephesians 4:26, 27 _____

_____

C. Ephesians 4:32 _____

_____

D. Psalm 141:3 _____

_____

E. Proverbs 12:25 _____

_____

F. Proverbs 15:1, 4 _____

_____

G. Proverbs 15:28 _____

_____

H. Proverbs 21:23 _____

_____

barriers to communication

1. To deepen love's dialogue, learn what interrupts effective communication.

Read the Scripture verses and comment briefly on what to avoid in communication.

A. Proverbs 11:12 _____

_____

B. Proverbs 11:13 _____

_____

C. Proverbs 12:16 _____

_____

D. Proverbs 12:18 _____

_____

E. Proverbs 12:22 _____

_____

F. Proverbs 18:2 _____

_____

G. Proverbs 18:13 _____

_____

H. Proverbs 21:19 _____

_____

I. Proverbs 29:20 _____

_____

Take a big step in improving your communication by vowing never to make your partner the object of remarks which cut, belittle, or ridicule!

2. Anger is real!

A. Circle the following statements about anger True or False.

1/ T F All human beings have the emotion of anger.

2/ T F Christians are not ever supposed to get angry.

3/ T F Silence can be an escape from settling angry feelings.

4/ T F Aggressive feelings should be recognized and resolved.

B. What does James 1:19, 20 say about anger?

_____

_____

_____

You may disagree with your partner but agree to disagree agreeably!

the tongue

James 3:1-12 talks about the control of the tongue. Look at this passage and then answer the following questions.

1. To what does God compare the tongue in verses 3-6?

_____

_____

2. How is the tongue described in verses 7 and 8?

_____

_____

3. What is the implication in verses 9-12? Check appropriate answers.

    A. ( ) To praise God and condemn man reveals inconsistency.

    B. ( ) Nature exhibits many contradictions.

    C. ( ) God's help is needed to control the tongue.

application

1. In order to strengthen communication in your marriage, try this experiment: Mentally switch roles and try to express your partner's feelings on the condition of your present communication relationship.

2. Now both husband and wife should tell his/her own desires for improving communication.

3. Agree on one area of increasing better communication immediately.

lesson 5

consideration— maturity in marriage

Your relationship with your mate is a marital or a martial one, depending on where you put the "I"!

The husband and wife who consistently place the happiness and well-being of the other partner ahead of personal desires find their marriage relationship considerably enriched.

"(Love) seeketh not her own" 1 Corinthians 13:5. This verse reveals the heart of the biblical principle of consideration and, when put into daily practice, is one of the best investments you can make in your marriage.

consideration—what is it?

1. What is your definition of "consideration"?

_____

_____

_____

_____

2. How do others define it? Get an opinion from someone else (also write down what others share during the study discussion time).

_____

_____

49

_____

_____

_____

3. Name some of the ways you feel maturity in marriage and consideration go together.

_____

_____

_____

_____

_____

_____

4. List some of the evidences of consideration which you feel have contributed to the success of marriages which you have observed.

_____

_____

_____

_____

_____

_____

basic scriptures

1. Ephesians 4:2: "Be humble and gentle. Be patient with each

other, making allowance for each other's faults because of your love." (*The Living Bible*)

A. From the list below, check the actions you feel would apply to "being humble and gentle."

    1/ (   ) To admit error in deed or attitude when wrong.

    2/ (   ) To wait for the other person to make amends first.

    3/ (   ) To look for ways to help the other partner.

    4/ (   ) To expect what is due one's self.

    5/ (   ) To consider timing before making requests.

B. What do you think is implied in "making allowance for each other's faults?"

_____

_____

_____

_____

_____

The following are all important. However, as you consider the challenge to "be patient with each other," which is most difficult for you to do?

    1/ To accede to the request of the other with no adverse comment.

    2/ To take time to think before responding.

    3/ Not to insist on having your own way.

    4/ Not to get upset when things don't go as you had planned.

Answer _____

Why? _____

_____

_____

_____

_____

2. Philippians 2:3, 4, "Let nothing be done through strife or vain-glory; but in lowliness of mind let each esteem other better than themselves. Look not every man on his own things, but every man also on the things of others." (King James Version)

A. This verse says to "count others better than ourselves."

Does this mean you have no rights? _____ What does it say to you?

_____

_____

_____

_____

B. In your marriage, how do you work out verse 4, "Not looking out for your own things or interests, but also the interests and things of your spouse?"

_____

_____

_____

_____

_____

C. What do you think "let nothing be done through strife or vainglory" means?

_____

_____

_____

_____

_____

Memorize and/or write out on a card Ephesians 4:2 or Philippians 2:3, 4 and put it on your desk, mirror in the bathroom, or above the kitchen sink —a place where you can think about what it means and work on putting it into practice.

simple guidelines

1. The Bible is full of wise counsel about being considerate. After each of the following verses, indicate the principle(s) of consideration you see in them.

A. Colossians 3:19 _____

_____

B. 1 Corinthians 13:4 _____

_____

C. 1 Peter 3:7 _____

_____

D. 1 Corinthians 7:3-5 _____

E. Galatians 5:26 _____

F. Romans 12:10 _____

2. The observance of good manners and common courtesies do not belong just to courtship days, but are equally important in marriage. How would you appraise yourself in the areas listed below?

A. Personal appearance _____

B. Courtesy (If you want to be treated like a king, treat her like a queen, and vice versa!) _____

C. Etiquette _____

D. Thoughtfulness about giving expressions of love and appreciation _____

application

There may be several areas that have come to mind during this study in which you recognize that you are not being adequately considerate of your partner. Which do you feel needs working on most?

Work out some way to check up on this, so that a week from now you can see how you are doing. You may ask someone to check up on you, jot it down on a calendar, or write yourself a note, but do *something* to make sure you will not let it slip by.

summary

Thoughtful consideration for each other is an essential ingredient which each partner must put into the making of a happy marriage.

Success in this area is not automatic, but has to be continually cultivated so as to become a natural response. Husbands and wives have the responsibility to give proof of their high regard for each other by giving careful attention to the details of courtesy. If this is not done, the tendency will be to grow careless and offend those with whom life is lived most intimately.

sex in marriage

When God created man and woman, male and female, the Genesis record states, "Behold, it was very good!" According to God's own wisdom and design, sexuality was ordained for the *propagation* of the human race, for *pleasure,* and for the *expression* of that kind of love between man and wife which nourishes true oneness.

Neither the distorted image of somber, negative Puritanism which formulated the philosophy of sex for many years, nor the "new morality" which throws off all sexual restraints and argues for total sexual "freedom" is an accurate picture of the teaching of the Bible. It is God's intention that the good gift of sex be clearly understood and thus be a unitive force in the marriage relationship.

purpose of sex in marriage

1. For Procreation

A. What was God's command in Genesis 1:27, 28 which involved Adam and Eve in the increase of mankind?

_____

_____

B. How does Genesis 4:1 indicate obedience to God's basic plan for procreation?

_____

_____

2. To Build Unity

A. As a basis for his ideas about marriage, Jesus emphatically quotes from the Old Testament in Matthew 19:5, 6 that "the two shall become one." How do you feel the physical union can *contribute* to fulfilling this oneness?

_____

_____

_____

_____

_____

B. The clearest direction in the New Testament regarding sexual adjustment in marriage is given in 1 Corinthians 7:2-5. After reading this passage, which of the following statements do you think are true? Where you agree, give a short comment as to why you agree.

1/ _____ Both husband and wife have sexual desires and needs that are to be met in marriage.

_____

_____

2/ _____ Marriage partners are to keep themselves solely for their mates.

_____

_____

3/ _____ Each partner is responsible to put the sexual needs of the other before his/her own.

_____

_____

4/ _____ Neither husband nor wife should refuse the other's request for intercourse.

_____

_____

5/ _____ Abstinence is to be by mutual consent.

_____

_____

6/ _____ Abstinence should not be of long duration.

_____

_____

7/ _____ Prolonged abstinence puts undue temptation before your mate.

_____

_____

3. For Pleasure

A. Proverbs 5:15-19 reveals another aspect of sex in marriage —to enhance the enjoyment of life together.
Summarize in a sentence or two the instructions God gives here to the husband.

_____

_____

_____

B. A husband and wife are to enjoy regular sexual experiences where each partner seeks to give pleasure and satisfaction to the other.

Why do you think mutual sexual fulfillment is possible only when there has been complete self-giving in the sexual act?

_____

_____

_____

C. Song of Solomon 7:6-10 is part of a dialogue between lovers. Put into your own words some of the things you see in this passage that indicates the pleasurableness of the physical relationship.

_____

_____

_____

_____

sanctity of sex

1. Paraphrase (rewrite in your own words) Hebrews 13:4

_____

_____

_____

_____

_____

_____

2. Promiscuity is revealed throughout the Scriptures as being inconsistent with holy living and contrary to God's will.
1 Thessalonians 4:3-8 gives a clear instruction about sexual accountability.

A. What is given as the first reason for abstinence from immorality?

_____

_____

B. "Sanctification" means "to be set apart." According to this passage, a man should be "set apart" to holiness and to his wife. Why do you feel this is particularly important?

_____

_____

_____

_____

C. Verses 4 and 5 indicate the right attitude toward sex. Check below the statements you feel correspond with these verses:

1/ _____ The main objective in marriage is to satisfy sexual desires.

2/ _____ Sex relations belong *within* marriage.

3/ _____ A man should have a wife to fulfill his sex desires.

4/ _____ People who know God should have a different attitude toward sex than those who do not know him.

D. Verses 6, 7, and 8 give the other reasons for avoiding immorality. What are they?

1/ _____

_____

2/ _____

_____

3/ _____

_____

3. What does God say about faithfulness in marriage in Malachi 2:13-15?

_____

_____

_____

_____

4. The desire to maintain purity of life before God caused Job, the Old Testament saint, to make an important covenant.

A. Record this vow given in Job 31:1-4

_____

_____

_____

B. What reason does he give for this course of action?

_____

_____

_____

The Bible often uses the Hebrew verb "to know" to describe the sexual love experience of husband and wife. "Knowing" means far more than objective information and intellectual recognition of a person. It means a mutual exchange of the deepest sort of knowledge possible about the loved one.

God protects love by confining sex to marriage, for marriage provides love its best opportunity to develop and mature. Sex destroys when it operates outside the plan for marriage, while sex relations practiced within this plan make married life rich and complete.

general guidelines

This lesson is not intended to be a handbook on sex techniques. The Bible passages given are meant to convey God's overall purposes, direction, and limitations for expressing your sexuality.

God leaves some things unsaid because they vary with each individual couple. It is right to be concerned about mutual sexual adjustment in *your* marriage and to give constant attention to learning the skills that will enrich your sex relations.

The following Scriptures are basic to fulfilling the needs of one another:

1. Acts 20:35 is not written regarding the subject of sex, but how would the principle given apply in sexual intimacy?

_____

_____

_____

2. Philippians 2:3, 4 deals with consideration. Relate it here to the physical relationship.

A. How would "selfishness" be harmful to the sex act?

_____

_____

_____

B. Would "count others better than yourself" apply? Explain your answer.

_____

_____

_____

C. How can you "consider the interest" of the other, particularly in contrast to your own desires?

_____

_____

3. One of the books of the Bible that specifically portrays wedded love is the Song of Solomon. This love poem has much to teach about the sexual side of marriage. Examine the following verses:

A. Song of Solomon 1:2. Should the love relationship be (check appropriate answers)

1/ _____ Physically expressed?

2/ _____ Exhilarating?

3/ _____ Indifferent?

4/ _____ Anticipated?

B. From Song of Solomon 1:13-16 several things can be deduced. Do you agree with these?

1/ Verbal expressions of love are a part of a satisfying sexual relationship.
Yes or No

2/ The closeness of physical intimacy requires personal cleanliness and attention to being as attractive as possible for the other.
Yes or No

3/ There is excitement and utter delight in the closeness of the other.
Yes or No

C. Song of Solomon 4:1-7 and 5:10-16 reveal a healthy appreciation of the human body God created. No embarrassment or shame darkens the delight each finds in the other.

Do you agree? _____

Explain your answer

_____

_____

_____

_____

application

Now is a good time to discuss the whole matter of sex with your mate. Take the time to get alone and face this subject openly and honestly.

Talk about your reactions to this study: share how you feel about your sex relationship.

If either of you lacks knowledge about any aspect of sex, plan to get at least one book to increase your understanding and therefore your enjoyment of sexuality.

Renew your marriage committal and exclusive love for one another. _____ Check when done.

male and female– complementary beings

"He who made them from the beginning made them male and female" Matthew 19:4.

"The two shall become one" Ephesians 5:31.

God chose to create two sexes. He purposed that men and women should complement and complete each other (not compete with one another!).

Neither sex is independent of the other; rather, they are interdependent according to 1 Corinthians 11:11, 12. "Nevertheless, in the Lord woman is not independent of man nor man of woman; for as woman was made from man, so man is now born of woman. And all things are from God." Each sex has equal dignity and is of unique worth to God. He has given you and your partner "maleness" and "femaleness" so that you can complete each other. As husband and wife you need to work out a system of roles and job assignments that will best suit you as individuals and your own marriage relationship. These responsibilities will have to be re-evaluated and adjusted from time to time as circumstances and needs change.

basic roles

A few roles in life are determined by one's sex. Genesis, "the book of beginnings," records the origin of man and gives many of these primary roles.

From each of the following Scriptures list the role given and check the gender to whom it applies. The first one is answered for you.

	ROLE Male-Female	MALE ✓	FEMALE ✓
1. Genesis 1:27	Male-Female	✓	✓
2. Genesis 1:28			
3. Genesis 2:15			
4. Genesis 2:18, 22			
5. Genesis 2:24			
6. Genesis 4:1			

scriptural interpretation of roles

Western culture implies that marriage is a unity created by romantic love and common interests. The Scriptures reveal that marriage is a unity created by God. A man and a woman, each with distinct personality, background, and experiences commit themselves to each other in marriage and become one in God's eyes.

In a Christian marriage, the partners look to God to learn how to best combine their differences and form a new identity. Since the Bible was given in part to instruct man in daily living, it contains a vast amount of truth about marriage and how to successfully maintain this all-important relationship.

1. Read Ephesians 5:21-33 carefully and answer the following questions about the passage.

A. According to verse 21, what attitude honors Christ?

_____

_____

B. By observing and following the example given in these

verses, a husband and wife can know how they are to relate to each other. What does verse 25 say concerning the responsibility of a husband to his wife?

_____

_____

_____

C. You can better understand *how* husbands are to love their wives as you see *how* Christ loved the church. From the passage, list the characteristics of Christ's love for the church. Then compile a list showing the husband's responsibility in loving his wife, using the same passage.

Christ, Head of the church	Husband, head of the wife
_____	_____
_____	_____
_____	_____
_____	_____
_____	_____
_____	_____

D. What do verses 22-24 say to wives?

_____

_____

_____

_____

_____

E. Read the statements below and check those which you believe to be accurate.

1/ _____ The husband has been appointed head of his wife and family, and by following her husband's leadership, a wife is being obedient to Christ.

2/ _____ A husband must possess strong leadership qualities and abilities or his wife is not expected to consider him head of their family.

3/ _____ The relationship between Christ and his bride, the church, illustrates the relationship which should exist between husband and wife.

4/ _____ A wife may retain the right to choose the areas in which she will be subject to her husband's leadership.

Using personal pronouns, put verse 33 in your own words.

_____

_____

2. Look at 1 Peter 3:1-7

A. What result can be expected when a wife lives in right relationship to her husband? verses 1, 2

_____

_____

_____

B. Do you agree with the following statements relating to verse 3-6? Check those you feel are correct.

1/ _____ A wife is not to be concerned with how she looks.

70

2/ _____ A wife's inner beauty is more important to God than her outer beauty.

3/ _____ It was the inner qualities of a gentle and quiet spirit that prompted Sarah to follow Abraham's leadership.

C. Read the admonition to husbands in verse 7. What does this verse say about

1/ *How* a husband is to live with his wife?

_____

_____

2/ *Why* a husband should know and understand his wife?

_____

_____

3/ *What* husband and wife share equally?

_____

_____

4/ *What* interferes with a husband's prayer life?

_____

_____

chain of command

1. Clearly spelled out in 1 Corinthians 11:3 is God's order of chain of command in life. When each one fulfills his function properly, there will be harmony in daily living as God intends it. What is the order given?

_____

_____

_____

_____

2. Ephesians 6:1 gives the relationship of the children in the chain of command. To whom are they responsible?

_____

3. *Humbling oneself is an act of the will.* Note in Philippians 2:5-11 how Jesus Christ willingly put himself under God's authority in order to secure man's redemption.

　A. What was Christ's position originally? verse 6

_____

_____

　B. What did he choose to do? verse 7, 8

_____

_____

　C. How did God honor his obedience? verse 9-11

_____

_____

4. According to 1 Peter 5:6 what will be the result of choosing to humble yourself?

_____

5. Proverbs 31:28-31 records the praise given to a wife by her family. Give a short summary of their remarks.

_____

_____

_____

6. In Genesis 18:17-19 God makes some remarks about Abraham. What was to be the outcome of this man's faithfulness?

_____

_____

_____

7. Is it difficult for you to humble yourself and take your proper place in God's chain of command?

_____

task assignments

Some tasks must be assigned in each marriage so that the daily life can run smoothly. These need not be thought of as being "feminine" or "masculine," but rather should be done by the partner best equipped to do the job. The responsibilities may be exchanged from time to time as circumstances change.

1. According to Titus 2:4, 5, who will generally be responsible for keeping the home?

_____

2. To whom does 1 Timothy 5:8 give the responsibility for seeing that the family is provided for?

_____

3. List some specific task assignments in your family and the person who is responsible for them, i.e. finances, dishes, purchases. Some may be shared assignments.

TASK   PERSON

_____   _____

_____   _____

_____   _____

_____   _____

4. Do you see when these may be changed in the future?

_____

_____

application

1. As you think through what you have learned about God's plan for roles in marriage, what do you see as the major need for readjustment in your marriage?

_____

_____

_____

2. Does your chain of command presently look like this?

Wife		Children		God-Christ
Husband	or this?	Husband-Wife	or this?	Husband
Children		Christ-God		Wife
Christ-God				Children

Check the one which is most like yours.

74

summary

Today traditional "roles" in marriage are being challenged—some rightly so! It is necessary to understand and apply scriptural principles in your marriage so you will not be confused by the prevailing ideas of society which may change tomorrow!

"The Lord commanded us to do all these statutes, to fear the Lord our God, *for our good always* . . ." Deuteronomy 6:24.

principles of partnership

"And the two shall become one flesh; consequently they are no longer two but one flesh. What therefore God has joined together, let no man separate" Mark 10:8, 9.

From courtship days "till death us do part," marriage partners must guard against that which could come between them.

Whenever anything, or anyone, poses a threat to "oneness," no matter how *good* it may seem, it is contrary to God's *best* for you and must be evaluated and placed in its proper perspective in your relationship.

In this lesson you will discover the importance of partnership at every stage of the life cycle of your marriage.

forming the partnership

Even though you may already be married, it is helpful to consider the courtship and engagement stage which are first steps toward establishing a relationship of growing oneness.

1. To the following list, add other things you feel should be a part of the engagement period.

A. Learning to understand and relate to each other.

B. Exploring attitudes and values toward life.

C. Planning details of the wedding.

D. _____

_____

E. _____

_____

F. _____

_____

G. _____

_____

H. _____

_____

2. The Scriptures give guidelines for the kind of relationship a couple considering marriage should have. What guidelines do you see in these passages?

A. 2 Corinthians 6:14, 15

_____

_____

_____

B. Amos 3:3

_____

_____

_____

C. 1 Thessalonians 4:3

_____

3. Genesis 29:16-20 records Jacob's love for Rachel. Write down the evidences of love you observe in these verses:

_____

_____

_____

_____

_____

_____

4. What do you think is a primary area of partnership that *should* have been worked on during your courtship and engagement period?

_____

_____

_____

partnership before parenthood

Marriage begins with the two of you and 20-25 years later, after child-rearing days are over, that is how it will be again—just the two of you! The early months and years of marriage are vitally important as you and your mate establish a new family system distinct from your background families. The arrival of children will add a new dimension to your relationship but when they later leave for homes of their own, you should be able to continue in unabated partnership.

1. Listed below are some of the major developmental tasks a couple faces in early years of marriage. Explain why you feel these adjustments are necessary for the growth of a marriage.

A. Adjusting to the realities of marriage (which can be disillusioning after the euphoria of courtship and engagement!)

_____

_____

_____

_____

_____

B. Adjusting to the emotional separation from parents and family while taking on a new role of husband or wife.

_____

_____

_____

_____

_____

C. Adjusting to faults and weaknesses in marriage partner

which may have been overlooked or ignored during courtship when mate was overidealized.

_____

_____

_____

_____

_____

D. Adjusting to knowledge that building a healthy marriage
requires time and effort.

_____

_____

_____

_____

_____

2. A family is the basic unit of society. Why do you feel this is true?

_____

_____

_____

_____

3. The relationship that exists between Christ and the church is
given in Ephesians 5:21-33 to show husbands and wives how to
relate happily to one another. Many principles that will develop

a gratifying partnership can be drawn from these verses. Complete the list given below:

A. Verse 21 _____

_____

B. Verses 22-24 A husband is to give loving leadership and protection to his wife.

C. Verse 25 _____

_____

_____

D. Verses 26, 27 A husband should desire to help his wife develop her full potential as a loved person.

E. Verses 28-30 _____

_____

_____

_____

F. Verse 31 A husband and wife should be more to each other than to anyone else in the world.

G. Verse 33 _____

_____

_____

_____

4. In your early marriage stage what was/is one of your adjustment needs?

_____

_____

_____

5. What was/is a stress point for your mate and how did/do you try to give support in this need?

_____

_____

_____

partnership and the family

Marriage is permanent! Child-rearing is only temporary. A person is not going to do much good in rearing children if he doesn't have the right relationship with his partner.

1. What are some ways a husband and wife can maintain their priority of commitment to each other when children come along?

A. _____

B. _____

C. _____

2. Why should parents present a "united front" to their children?

A. _____

B. _____

C. _____

3. What are some dangers *for parents* who overinvest in their children and underinvest in their marriage?

_____

_____

_____

_____

4. How would this affect *the children?*

_____

_____

_____

_____

5. What is your impression of your parents' partnership during your growing-up years?

_____

_____

_____

6. What lesson can you learn from their relationship?

_____

_____

_____

partnership in the middle years and beyond

1. There are more divorces after 20 years of marriage than any

other time except during the first three years. What do you think contributes to the failure of partnership at this stage?

A. _____

_____

B. _____

_____

C. _____

_____

2. According to Song of Solomon 8:7, how enduring should love be?

_____

_____

3. How can couples help each other prepare for the child-leaving stage?

A. Husband can help wife by . . .

_____

_____

_____

B. Wife can help husband by . . .

_____

_____

_____

4. What are some of the opportunities for enjoyment during the "empty nest" years?

A. Proverbs 17:6 _____

B. Ecclesiastes 9:9 _____

C. Philippians 3:13, 14 _____

_____

5. As you examine your present relationship to your mate, what area of partnership do you see that needs strengthening to meet the needs of middle-years crisis?

_____

_____

_____

summary

Partnership is more important than parenthood. How one treats and loves his marriage partner · is going to determine what he will do with his family.

lesson 9

pattern for parenthood

It has been said that *two* are never more *one* than when they become *three!*

This unusual math equation has an element of truth in it, as most marriage partners discover when their first baby is born.

Although child-raising imposes new responsibilities and pressures on your marriage, the Bible provides clear instructions to help you do the job.

Remember that a husband and wife who have a mutually satisfying and growing relationship themselves already possess one important requirement for successful parenthood.

points to ponder

Do you think the following statements are true or false? Circle your answer, then give a brief reason for your choice:

1.   T   F   One dare not sacrifice his (her) marriage partner for his (her) children.

_____

_____

_____

2.   T   F   The most potent influence on a child's future marriage is his observation of his parents' marriage.

_____

_____

_____

_____

3. T F Because of his many responsibilities, a husband should delegate most of the training of their children to his wife.

_____

_____

_____

4. T F The Word of God—"thus saith the Lord"—should be the authoritative base upon which decisions regarding family living are made.

_____

_____

_____

5. T F Children should be allowed to decide for themselves if they want religious training.

_____

_____

_____

birth control in christian marriages

Birth control is not a basic moral issue. The Bible gives no clear or definite word for or against it. When the Scriptures do not speak clearly and positively on a specific subject, it must then be decided on the basis of scriptural *principles*. These must be honestly applied by each one with a desire to discover and fulfill God's will for the individual family.

What guidelines and principles concerning family planning do you see in the following passages:

1. Genesis 1:28 _____

_____

_____

2. Psalm 127:3-5 _____

_____

_____

3. 1 Timothy 5:8 _____

_____

_____

4. James 1:5 _____

_____

_____

5. 1 Peter 3:7 _____

_____

_____

If birth control is employed, a couple must find agreement of attitude and purpose, resulting in a shared conclusion, and employ a method satisfying to both parties.

preparing for parenthood

Co-creating a child is a short-term biological process! Molding the character of that child takes long years of thoughtful teaching and training.

Preparation for child-rearing requires more than a vague hope that everything will work out all right. As in all other areas of life, you must learn to accomplish right goals by an exercise of your *will*, not by emotions. Emotions can and do enter in, but emotions can be misleading. Successful parenting requires determination, preparation, planning, prayer—and hard work!

Here are some basic guidelines:

1. Review the chain of command which God has established for the family as given in 1 Corinthians 11:3 and Ephesians 6:1.

_____

_____

2. List what you feel is involved in fulfilling Deuteronomy 6:6, 7.

_____

_____

_____

_____

3. Since the home is the primary source of Christian education and training, how would you put Proverbs 22:6 into practice?

_____

_____

_____

4. It has been said that parents too often "major" on "minors" when it comes to training children.

A. List several character traits that you feel are necessary to develop in your child's personality.

Example 1/ obedience _____

2/ _____

3/ _____

4/ _____

5/ _____

6/ _____

7/ _____

B. What are some areas of lesser importance that you feel can be overemphasized by parents?

Example 1/ overly concerned with clothes children wear

2/ _____

3/ _____

4/ _____

developing character

The basis of Christian character is the life of Christ living in the Christian.

The goal in the mind of a parent should be to

lead his child to a personal encounter with and faith in the Son of God.

This commitment to Jesus Christ will enable a child to develop goodness of character.

From birth to "rebirth in Christ" your child's character foundation is built by the relationships and examples he observes in his home.

If you as a parent know God's teaching on character development, you can lead your child in the way of truth.

1. What does God want in his people?
Match references with characteristics listed below:

Example A. obedience to God _____k_____ a. 1 John 4:7

      B. obedience to parents _____b. Philippians 2:3, 4

      C. truthfulness _____c. Matthew 22:37

      D. faith in God _____d. Acts 20:35

      E. purity (holiness) _____e. Ephesians 4:25

      F. integrity _____f. 1 Thessalonians 4:3, 7

      G. honesty _____g. 2 Corinthians 8:21

      H. love for God _____h. Hebrews 11:6

      I. love for others _____i. Proverbs 12:22

      J. humility _____j. Colossians 3:20

      K. generosity _____k. John 14:15

2. What should you do when you have a question concerning situations and choices not explicitly dealt with in the Bible? You can receive guidance by applying the following scriptural principles.

Indicate what these are:

A. 1 Corinthians 6:12 _____

_____

_____

B. 1 Corinthians 8:13 _____

_____

C. 1 Corinthians 10:31 _____

_____

D. Acts 24:16 _____

_____

_____

3. Family worship offers an ideal setting for further development of character. The scriptural admonition to parents is to represent God to their children and to present their children to God.
As a family gathers together to worship in his presence, there is no one set pattern that should be followed. Remember, "the shorter the child, the shorter the devotions!"
From the following list of possible activities for family worship, check those which you have tried:

A. Bible reading
B. Singing
C. Dramatization of Bible stories
D. Scripture memorization
E. Praying
F. Reading of Christian books and biographies
G. Records or tapes
H. Others

application

Are you concerned about building the right kind of character traits into your children? Ephesians 6:4 instructs fathers to "bring children up in the discipline and instruction of the Lord."

What steps are you taking to insure that these godly characteristics will be developed?

_____

_____

_____

_____

_____

_____

_____

_____

lesson 10

training—
the development of the child

"No greater joy can I have than this, to hear that my children follow the truth" 3 John 4.

The challenging task of raising children will occupy many years of married life for most couples. Partners can grow together on a new and different level as they share the responsibilities and joys of bringing their children to maturity.

The goal and prayer of Christian parents is to guide their children so that they will "increase in wisdom and stature, and in favor with God and man" Luke 2:52.

train — by example

Telling is not *teaching!* *Listening* is not *learning!*

Parents teach more by *example* than by *precept* because children tend to *imitate* what they *see* rather than do what they hear, if there is a conflict between the two.

1. Consult a dictionary and write a short definition of the word "train" as it applies to rearing children.

_____

_____

_____

2. Read Genesis 18:19 and note God's instructions to Abraham. Then consider the following statements and circle the answers you feel are correct.

A.   T   F   Abraham was to *suggest* to his family that they follow the Lord.

B.   T   F   Abraham was an example of right living to his household.

C.   T   F   God left the decision to Abraham as to what he was to do.

D.   T   F   God wanted to fulfill his promise to Abraham. This would be determined by Abraham's obedience.

3. In writing to the church at Philippi (Philippians 4:9), what did the Apostle Paul say would be the result of following his example?

_____

_____

4. What are some of the things Timothy observed about Paul's life as recorded in 2 Timothy 3:10, 11?

_____

_____

_____

According to 2 Timothy 1:5
5. Who served as examples to Timothy when he was a child?

_____

6. What was one means of instruction for Timothy? 2 Timothy 3:15

_____

7. Paul reminded Timothy (in 1 Timothy 4:12) that he had a responsibility to set an example for others to follow. List below the areas of example given in this passage. Note beside each a specific way you can be an example to your children in that area.

_____   _____

_____   _____

_____   _____

_____   _____

_____   _____

In Galatians 6:7 the Bible cautions that "whatever a man sows, that will he also reap." To a great degree you will reproduce your own life in your children. If a child is given good instruction while at the same time a bad example is set for him, confusion will result. Therefore, if your child is to *be* the right kind of person you must be sure that your life is an example of what you teach.

train — by instruction

An important responsibility of parents is to interpret life to their children. If possible, information and principles should be taught when rules are given. Rules tell your child *what* to do but it is needful to help him to develop his own reasoning capacity by teaching him *why*.

1. Deuteronomy 6:4-7 carefully instructs parents in their responsibility towards their children. As you consider these verses, complete the following:

A. As parents, my mate and I are to be wholehearted in our own response to _____

B. The Word of God is to be in my _____

C. This is not an option but a _____

D. We should _____ them _____ to our children.

E. We should teach our children the Word when we _____

_____ and _____ and _____

and _____

2. Look up Proverbs 22:6 and write this promise of God in your own words.

_____

_____

_____

_____

3. Luke 2:52 records of Jesus Christ that he grew mentally, physically, spiritually and socially. Each of the following verses relates to one of these four areas. Give the key thought of the passage and name the heading, or headings, under which it fits. The first one is answered for you.

Passage	Key Thought	Heading
A. Matthew 19:13, 14	Little children can know Jesus	Spiritually
B. Proverbs 1:5	_____	_____
C. Proverbs 23:12	_____	_____
D. 2 Peter 3:18	_____	_____
E. Judges 13:24	_____	_____
F. 1 Samuel 2:26	_____	_____

4. With your partner, evaluate your children in the light of the above four areas. List below the name of each child. Determine his area of greatest need, and give one thing you can do to help him grow.

Child's Name	Area of Need	What We Can Do About It

train — by love and discipline

Love and discipline are the foundation of training your child. Love is essential from infancy through growing years. It would be difficult for your child to become a happy, emotionally secure person without generous amounts of love! Without discipline you can not hope to teach your child to be a respectful, competent and responsible adult. There is no greater proof of your love than correctly applied admonition and/or discipline and it reveals your willingness to risk personal rejection (at least for a time!) for the welfare of your child.

1. Read 1 Samuel 3:12, 13. Why was Eli held accountable for the wrongdoing of his sons?

_____

_____

_____

2. Note the subject of discipline in Hebrews 12:5-11—then put a check after the following statements which you feel to be accurate.

A. The Lord never chastens anyone. _____

B. The chastening of the Lord is directly related to his love. _____

C. Disciplining is for the good of the one disciplined. _____

D. Discipline is pleasurable for all concerned. _____

E. The purpose of administering discipline is to produce a right quality of living. _____

3. Proverbs 3:11, 12 gives similar insight concerning discipline. What should discipline reveal about the parent's relationship to his child?

_____

_____

4. What principle of discipline is given in Ecclesiastes 8:11?

_____

_____

5. Ephesians 6:4 gives guidelines for parents seeking to mold the character of their children.

A. What does this verse say a father is to *do*?

_____

_____

B. What is a father to *avoid* doing?

_____

_____

C. List three things a father could do which would "provoke his children to anger." (You might want to get some ideas from your children!)

1/ _____

_____

2/ _____

_____

3/ _____

_____

6. The proverbs of Solomon were written that men may "know wisdom and instruction" and "understand words of insight" (Proverbs 1:2). What do you think each of the following passages is saying about discipline?

A. Proverbs 13:24 _____

_____

_____

B. Proverbs 19:18 _____

_____

_____

C. Proverbs 20:11 _____

_____

_____

D. Proverbs 29:15 _____

_____

E. Proverbs 29:17 _____

7. As you read 1 Corinthians 13:4-7, 11, think about your relationship with your children.

A. Do you think you exhibit the kind of love to them that this passage describes? Yes _____ No _____

B. Do you think you give each of your children adequate attention and time? Yes _____ No _____

C. Do you have a tendency to substitute material "things" for giving of yourself? Yes _____ No _____

D. Do your expectations of your children fit their ages? Yes _____ No _____

E. Do your children seem to enjoy their relationship with you? Yes _____ No _____

> Your child should understand that his parents · are themselves under God's authority and are accountable to him. Parents make mistakes, and children know it! If you err in disciplining him in anger, wrong judgment or application, confess your fault to your child and ask for his forgiveness. He will learn to do this too . . . both with you and with God!
>
> You may be starting late to apply God's principles of training. Your children may be older . . . and rebellious. Don't be discouraged; start now! "For with God nothing shall be impossible" Luke 1:37.

atmosphere of the home

There is a difference between a house and a home!

A house is a building in which people live. A home is a place dear to one because of personal relationships, feelings of comfort and security, or warmth and fellowship: not only a place of personal attachment, but a refuge from the demands of life.

A happy home does not depend upon material comforts for satisfaction as much as it does upon the atmosphere that is created by the family itself.

the family as a unit

A family is the total of what its members are individually, plus their interrelationships one with another. The family is the basic unit of society.

1. What fact concerning families do you see in this verse? "So Noah went forth, and his sons and his wife and his sons' wives with him. And every beast, every creeping thing, and every bird, everything that moves upon the earth, went forth *by families* out of the ark" Genesis 8:18, 19 RSV

_____

_____

_____

2. The account of a census taken by Moses and Aaron is given in Numbers 1:17-19. How was the congregation registered?

_____

hindrances to family unity

Many forces in modern living combine to threaten the "togetherness" of the family life. The home is no longer the center of recreation, education, worship, or production of goods. Thus it is difficult to maintain common interests which involve all its members.

1. Make a simple evaluation of the time your family has spent *together* in the past week (other than at mealtime). Give approximate amount of time for each day.

Sunday —————————————————————

Monday —————————————————————

Tuesday —————————————————————

Wednesday —————————————————————

Thursday —————————————————————

Friday —————————————————————

Saturday —————————————————————

2. Families today are very mobile! Few adults live in the same city as grandparents, parents, or other relatives, or have much close contact with them. How do you think this social change affects you and your children?

——————————————————————————————

——————————————————————————————

——————————————————————————————

——————————————————————————————

creating the atmosphere

"By wisdom a house is built, and by understanding it is established; by knowledge the rooms are filled with all precious and pleasant riches" Proverbs 24:3, 4.

1. Like the spokes of a wheel, the closer family members are to the Hub (Christ), the closer they are to each other.

A. What commitment did Joshua make for his family in Joshua 24:15?

_____

_____

B. The reality of the parents' relationship to Jesus Christ will prepare their children for faith in him. What does 1 John 1:3 say will be the result?

_____

_____

_____

C. What is the source of family strength, according to Psalm 127:1?

_____

_____

D. This is a good time to review the study you did on the

subject of family worship in Lesson 9. Describe what this means in the light of the atmosphere of your home.

_____

_____

_____

_____

_____

2. According to Colossians 3:12-15 what ten things should characterize relationships in a Christian family?

A. _____

B. _____

C. _____

D. _____

E. _____

F. _____

G. _____

H. _____

I. _____

J. _____

3. Each quality listed above interacts with all the others. How would you explain the relationship between:

A. Forgiveness and peace _____

_____

_____

_____

B. Compassion and kindness _____

_____

_____

_____

C. Forbearance and patience _____

_____

_____

_____

> The ability to forgive and accept forgiveness graciously is a necessity for building good relationships in the family life. More important than fixing blame in a disagreement is the *attitude* of the people involved. It is difficult to say, "Forgive me" or "I forgive you" without putting any conditions on the statement!

As a practical application for this lesson, what specific steps can you take to make genuine forgiveness a day-by-day part of your marriage?

_____

_____

_____

_____

_____

4. What facts concerning the atmosphere in the home do you see in the following Scriptures?

A. Psalm 133:1 _____

_____

B. Proverbs 15:17 _____

_____

C. Proverbs 17:1 _____

_____

D. Proverbs 17:22 _____

_____

E. Proverbs 25:24 _____

_____

F. Mark 3:25 _____

_____

5. Here are three other areas to be considered as you analyze your home situation.

A. It is important that your home be attractively kept and a pleasant place to live.

B. It is important that there be a balance between group spirit and individuality so that each family member can mature as a unique person.

C. It is important that a family *enjoy* life together. Family activities and home life should include a lot of laughter, fun, and games!

As you reflect on your childhood days, which of these elements were present in your family life? How did this affect you as a person?

_____

_____

_____

_____

the home and hospitality

The Scriptures place much emphasis upon the value of keeping an "open house" with a glad heart.

Consider each Scripture, then write down anything in the passage related to hospitality.

1. Romans 12:13 _____

_____

2. Hebrews 13:2 _____

_____

3. 3 John 5-8 _____

_____

4. Matthew 25:34-45 _____

_____

summary

Your home must be more than a place to eat and sleep if it is to fulfill its intended mission! The basic emotions—the desire to be loved, to be secure, to be needed, and to belong—are best nurtured in the relationships of the family.

money--friend or foe?

There is no question about money being a necessary factor in modern society. Money and choices about its use are a daily part of married life.

Money can mean many different things to people. Money not only has the power to buy the necessities of life but can also symbolize a measure of success, power, social status, or emotional security. The Christian couple who acknowledges the Lordship of Christ over all of their lives, including money, must be careful to *use* money and not let it use them!

basic attitudes toward money

The fundamental teaching of the Scriptures about money is that of *stewardship*. A steward is one who manages *another's* property or financial affairs which have been entrusted to his care. Since God is the original supplier of all you possess, you are accountable to him to manage your resources well.

1. From what source does wealth come, according to Deuteronomy 8:17, 18 and 1 Chronicles 29:12?

_____

_____

_____

2. How should you feel about all that God gives you? Ecclesiastes 5:19 and 1 Timothy 6:17.

_____

_____

3. Put Ecclesiastes 5:10 in your own words:

_____

_____

_____

_____

4. One of the strongest admonitions concerning money is found in 1 Timothy 6:6-10. The statement, "You can't take it with you!" comes from this passage. What other truths about money do you observe here?

A. _____

B. _____

C. _____

D. _____

5. In Luke 12:13-21
   A. Why did Jesus caution against covetousness? (Verse 15)

_____

_____

B. Why do you think God called the rich man a fool?

_____

C. What application of the parable did Jesus make? (Verse 21)

_____

_____

6. Hebrews 13:5 encourages valuing God's priorities rather than man's. What warning do you see in this verse?

_____

_____

_____

7. What secret had Paul learned that enabled him to be content regardless of his financial state? Philippians 4:11-13

_____

_____

_____

The attitude of the heart toward God first and then toward possession is what is most important in God's sight. This will eliminate the ever-present danger of placing your trust in your resources rather than in God.

8. Do you feel you and your mate have acknowledged Christ as Lord of your financial life? _____ Explain your answer:

_____

_____

_____

using money wisely

Family management of money requires thoughtful effort to avoid problems. Here are some basic principles regarding earning and spending money.

1. How will most of the necessities for a family be provided? 2 Thessalonians 3:7-12

_____

_____

2. What practical example does Proverbs 6:6-8 give for consideration?

_____

_____

_____

3. Taxes are a very real part of life today. What do the following verses teach about them?

A. Romans 13:6, 7 _____

_____

B. Matthew 17:24-27 _____

_____

C. Matthew 22:15-22 _____

_____

4. What should the character of a Christian steward reveal? 1 Corinthians 4:1, 2

_____

5. What does Proverbs 22:7 say is the relationship of a borrower to a lender?

6. What do these verses teach about the financial responsibility family members have for one another?

A. Matthew 15:1-6 _____

B. 2 Corinthians 12:14 _____

C. 1 Timothy 5:8 _____

7. A budget is an estimate of what a family's income and expenses will be and a couple who want a realistic guide for planning and spending will find it absolutely essential to prepare one. Do you and your mate have a workable plan for handling your finances?

how to give

Jesus said, "It is more blessed to give than to receive" Acts 20:35. Every couple needs to evaluate carefully how and where their financial support will be given.

1. 2 Corinthians 8:5 records for Christians the first principle of giving. What is it?

2. As you read 2 Corinthians 9:6-12, note some other principles concerning giving. Add to the list given below:

A. Giving should be a matter of personal conviction. _____

B. Giving should be a joy for the giver. _____

C. _____

D. _____

E. _____

F. _____

3. Mark 12:41-44 tells of Jesus observing a widow contributing to the temple treasury.

A. Why did he praise her? _____

_____

B. How did others contribute? _____

_____

4. What will be the result of giving with false motives? Matthew 6:1-4

_____

_____

5. To whom should you give?

A. Deuteronomy 15:10, 11 _____

B. Galatians 6:6; 1 Corinthians 9:11, 14

_____

C. 1 John 3:17, 18 _____

6. Malachi 3:10 states an Old Testament view of giving with which 1 Corinthians 16:2 agrees.
Check the following list as you note each statement in these verses.

A. _____ Giving should be planned

B. _____ Giving should be done at a regular time

C. _____ Giving should be proportional to income

D. _____ Giving is rewarded by God

7. What does Philippians 4:15-19 promise those who give to the Lord's work?

_____

_____

8. Are you satisfied with the system your family now has for channeling funds for giving?

_____

summary

Whether one or both partners contribute to the family income, it is important to operate in a "*we*" relationship: "*our*" money, not "*my*" money! Recognize that when possible each mate should have *some* money for personal needs and desires. After discussion, agreement should be made regarding the handling of finances, remembering that in this area, as in all others, God ultimately holds the husband responsible as head of the home.

Many conflicts about money can be avoided if marriage partners are familiar with specific areas of financial responsibility and come to a mutual decision regarding them.

In addition to the motives and actions studied in this lesson, you and your mate may need to reach an understanding about the areas listed below:

Put a check beside the ones you have already discussed:

_____ Setting a Christ-centered living standard

_____ Credit buying

_____ Spending for recreation

_____ Children's future education

_____ Insurance plans

_____ Making a will

_____ Savings and investments

_____ Long-term financial planning

lesson 13

other priority relationships

"My purpose is to give life in all its fullness"—
Jesus Christ (John 10:10, TLB).

For better or for worse, the quality of a marriage colors the total life of the partners.

The healthy closeness of a Christ-centered marriage should extend far beyond the four walls of the home to enrich the community—and the world.

The purpose of this series of lessons has been to focus on basic priorities: to God, to your mate, and to your family. These relationships must be maintained, in their proper perspective, with other spheres of responsibility that are a part of life.

A brief look at three of these areas will be helpful as you complete this final lesson.

your job and your employer

1. What principles do 2 Thessalonians 3:10, 12 and Genesis 3:19 have in common?

_____

_____

_____

2. Romans 13:7 concerns one's responsibility to governing authorities, but how could it be applied to your responsibility to an employer?

_____

3. Ephesians 6:5-9 gives instructions to employees and employers. Read the passage, and then circle either true or false the statements below.

A. T F   I am to do my work as "unto the Lord."

B. T F   I am responsible to obey those for whom I work.

C. T F   My objective at work is to impress my employer.

D. T F   The attitude I maintain at work is not important.

E. T F   God is not particularly interested in the quality job I do.

F. T F   As an employer I am responsible to God for the kind of "boss" I am to my employees.

4. How can you best do your work as "unto the Lord"? Draw at least three conclusions from Titus 2:9, 10.

A. _____

B. _____

C. _____

5. Why is it important to have a wholehearted attitude toward your job? 1 Corinthians 10:31.

_____

_____

_____

     A word of caution concerning your job may be needful. A person who *neglects* his family, however successful he may be before the world, is a failure with God. Some husbands (and some wives) give their family everything—everything but themselves!

your church

The Christian home does not stand alone but is part of a larger family. The church is God's family of families. Although parents hold and share the prime responsibility for the spiritual nurture of their children, they soon recognize that they need input from other sources. The local church can give this encouragement and in so doing undertakes the task of *supplementing* parental instruction and training.

1. A great many church members attend worship services *only* "for the sake of the children." There are other sound reasons given in Scripture for congregating with the family of God.
From the following Scriptures indicate these reasons.

A. Acts 8:25 _____

_____

B. Acts 20:28 _____

_____

C. 1 Corinthians 11:23-26 _____

_____

D. Ephesians 4:11-13 _____

_____

E. Hebrews 10:24, 25 _____

_____

2. What definition does your dictionary give for "worship" as it relates to God?

_____

_____

3. List some of the activities you enter into in the performance of *worship* at your church.

A. _____

B. _____

C. _____

D. _____

4. Acts 2:42 records the four most basic activities of the early church as they met together. Using your own words, describe what they did.

A. _____

B. _____

C. _____

D. _____

5. What should you expect from the leaders of your church? Fill in the blanks.

Jeremiah 3:15 says that "shepherds" (spiritual leaders) are to feed those in their care with _____ and _____.

1 Peter 5:2-4 exhorts them to tend (guard, guide, care for) those in their charge, not _____ but _____. In

all that they do they are to be _____ to the flock.

6. What responsibility does God put on those in the church as Hebrews 13:7, 17 records it?

A. The general congregation: _____

_____

_____

B. The leaders: _____

_____

_____

> Although the family and the local church should have a strong relationship to one another, care should again be exercised lest involvement become so heavy there is little time for the family itself to be together!

personal ministry

1. Matthew 5:16 indicates an important aspect of your daily life. *What* do you think this verse is saying?

_____

_____

_____

Explain *how* you think this could be accomplished.

_____

_____

_____

_____

2. What do the following passages say about a Christian's responsibilities to those around him?

A. Mark 16:15 _____

_____

B. 2 Corinthians 5:18-20 _____

_____

_____

C. Colossians 1:28, 29 _____

_____

_____

D. Matthew 28:18-20 _____

_____

_____

E. 2 Timothy 2:2 _____

_____

_____

3. The admonition to "make disciples" requires knowing what is involved in *being* a disciple. Use your dictionary to define the word "disciple." Record your findings.

_____

_____

_____

4. Discover what the Scriptures teach about discipleship. Record
your findings below.

A. Luke 9:23 _____

_____

_____

B. John 8:31 _____

_____

_____

C. John 13:34, 35 _____

_____

_____

D. John 15:8 _____

_____

_____

E. Luke 6:46 _____

_____

_____

As a result of this study on discipleship, what has God said to you?

_____

_____

_____

What will you do in response?

_____

_____

Be sure your personal ministry to others is in perspective to your time with your family.

stewardship of time

A common problem facing the modern family is the pressure of time.

The question of how individual family members can meet the demands for involvement in the community and still maintain good communications with one another is not easily answered.

1. A biblical injunction regarding the use of your time is found in Ephesians 5:15-17. Complete the list below relating to this verse.

A. I must be careful how I act.

B. I must exercise wisdom in my life.

C. _____

D. _____

E. _____

2. James states that a man's life is short and uncertain (James

4:14). In light of this knowledge, write Psalm 90:12 in your own words as a prayer request to God.

_____

_____

_____

_____

_____

Your life is continually undergoing change, making it necessary to keep close watch on your progress in maintaining your priority relationships.

The purpose of these lessons has been to provide a means by which you can better understand the marriage relationship from God's perspective.

A *perfect* marriage does not exist! But as you and your mate *apply* God's Word to your lives, he will enable you to experience all that was intended when "Two Become One."